How To Rescue Feral Cats

Discovering the Joy of Providing a Forever Home to Homeless Feral Cats in Need of Rescue

By

Carol-Ann Kennedy

Introduction

I want to thank you and congratulate you for buying the book **How to Rescue Feral Cats**.

This book contains proven steps and strategies on how to help homeless and feral cats in your community through safe, loving, and humane treatment. With the skills learned in this book you can turn your community's problem of feral cat overpopulation into a triumph of care and concern!

In this book you will learn how to care for feral cats in a way that makes them a benefit to the community that they live in! In this book you can learn about the Trap-Neuter-Return method, the right mindset for feral care, feeding, sheltering, and more! Every community has feral cats. Every community has cat lovers. Now with this book you will be equipped to begin making a real difference in the lives of feral cats and in the attitude of your neigbourhood toward these precious furry little animals.

Thanks again for buying this book. I hope you enjoy it!

Table of Contents

CHAPTER ONE: The Feral Cat Versus The Stray Cat

Many people think that "stray cat" and "feral cat" are interchangeable terms when really, there are vast differences between the two. While stray, feral and domestic (pet) cats are all the same genetically and are biologically connected to an extent, there are notable differences between their characters and natures.

Stray cats are pet cats that were, at one point, owned and taken care of by people in their home. They have been exposed to human touch and have been tamed and socialized, and have become reliant on owners for food and shelter. The cat will become a stray through abandonment by its owners, or possibly straying too far from home and becoming lost. A stray cat can, after a long period of time away from humans, become feral. They may also end up in feral colonies as a means of survival, or as a result of being dumped.

A true feral cat has never had any kind of human contact and is not socialized. Most feral cats are born feral. By this we mean that they are born into a feral colony and do not, from birth, have any contact with humans. In fact, people are seen by feral cats as a threat, and are often avoided all together. Most feral cats will run into hiding places such as bushes or storm drains if approached by people. The most fundamental difference between a feral cat and a stray cat, is that even if a stray cat becomes somewhat feral it can be re-socialised with the right treatment and rehabilitation. It is very highly unlikely that a true feral cat will ever be tame enough to become a domestic pet. A feral kitten, however, if young enough, can be socialised with care and patience.

CHAPTER TWO: Capture, Sterilization and Return of Feral Cats

There are various reasons as to why capturing and relocating feral cats is important. The most important being sterilization. Cats can reproduce at an unbelievable rate. To put this into perspective, an unsterilized female cat averaging a lifespan of around 7 years, will produce around 100 kittens in her lifetime, assuming that each year she produces 6 surviving kittens. So if a colony begins with 20 cats, this number over the course of seven years will be massively increased to around 2000 cats! Overpopulation is a huge problem - and the problem more than likely starts with domestic or previously owned cats. If a female is not spayed and is impregnated by a roaming, unneutered tomcat, many things could happen which will add to the problem of overpopulation, as well as unwanted kittens. Over population gives way to numerous problems which affect the welfare and safety of feral cats. One of the worst is cruelty. Feral cats can often be seen as pests and there have been far too many accounts of severe abuse inflicted on them. Feral cats in suburban areas become a problem if they become involved in fighting with domestic cats, especially during mating seasons.

The Capture-Neuter-Return of Feral Cats (also known as Trap-Neuter-Return or TNR) is an option that helps these furry animals live quiet, happy and peaceable lives alongside the human population. **The advantage of the TNR program is that it** ends the reproductive cycle of the cats. As you may know, cats reproduce with much greater frequency and litter size than do dogs. Because of this, a feral cat colony can grow at an alarming rate from year to year. While the process of TNR deals with the problem that many communities face with an over population of feral cats, it also improves the overall well-being of the cat. The stress, noise, and behavioural changes associated with mating and pregnancy of the cat stop the minute TNR is administered.

There are a number of organizations that gladly teach the principles and processes of TNR to those who want to help these feral cats. Those who work with feral and abandoned cats in your area would be the best source of practical information regarding best practices in your area. These organizations (if they exist in your town) can be found with a simple Google or Facebook search. If a person cannot attend the sessions held by these organizations for any reason, a concise guide like this one, will answer many of your questions. With time and experience, you will gain the confidence you need to correctly handle these shy beings

Now it is important for you to understand that many preparations must be made before you go out into the field and actually endeavour to trap feral cats. These preparations should start about two weeks before the actual date of capture.

Tasks you ensure you do before capturing these animals are:

> Put together a team. Find people who share the same passion for cats as you

have and together go through this book and take advantage of any learning opportunities with local feral/abandoned cat groups in your area. With the help of your team the expeditions into the world of helping these cats will be easier to handle.

➤ Maintain a book on each cat and kitten that you feed. One of the observations that you need to put into that book about every cat is if it is friendly or fearful of the humans around. It is also important to note which cats get along with each other, and any and all health related issues that will have to be addressed.

➤ Buy or borrow traps. Cats are trapped in the same traps that are used for the live capture of small animals such as large squirrels and racoons. These traps can be bought at most of the larger hardware stores or farm supply stores. They may not have these items on the store shelves but they usually have the access to suppliers and can have them ordered in for you.

Alternatively, you could order the traps online and have them delivered.

➢ Set and begin a feeding schedule for the cats at least 2 weeks in advance. Food should be placed in the traps themselves so that the cats gets used to walking into the traps to eat. Of course, you don't set the traps at this point yet.

➢ Ensure that each cat trap is strategically placed so that it is not in the way of or a danger to humans or traffic.

➢ Preparing for bringing the cats home is important. Your holding area or recovery area should be ready well in advance. Make use of a clean, well contained area in which the cats can recover after their surgeries. You need to make sure that the doors and windows of the recovery area can be securely closed before you keep the cat there. Please remember that cats – especially hurting and scared cats – can be very quick. It is wise to have a recovery area that opens into a secondary containment area (such as a closed hallway or another room) so that the cats cannot get out of their traps, run by you, and escape before it is their time to be released.

➤ Take time to make a list of all the equipment you need to take on the day that you are going to trap the cats.

➤ Make an appointment at the vet for neutering the cats well in advance.

➤ Do not feed the cats for twenty-four hours before trapping. Continue giving them water but no food. This will make sure they are hungry when you bait the traps on the big day.

➤ Please do not trap the cat on a day of extreme weather (heat/cold). It can prove fatal to the cat.

CHAPTER THREE: The Big Day

A person with experience in TNR will tell you "Well begun is half done". So, you need to ensure that everything is set in order and well organized before you actually venture into the field to trap the cats.

There are a few things that are important to note here.

- ➤ Make sure you prepare all the traps (bait them and set them) away from the colony. Tape newspaper to the bottom of the trap so that it covers well and tag every trap with numbers that you can later assign to the cats that are trapped.
- ➤ All the traps, especially the doors, should function properly. Bait every trap with adequate amount of food. You need to put a little food at the entrance of the trap and some food at the end of the trap. The bait should have a strong smelling fish odour that will attract the cat.

- Once you put the out the baited traps walk away and watch from a distance. You will need to be extremely patient. A feral cat, no matter how hungry, is a very cautious animal. He will take his time entering the trap.
- Once the cat is trapped, immediately cover the trap with a large towel before moving it. This will help calm the cat. An easier option would be to put a towel on top of the trap before putting it on the ground. This way, you would just need to cover the door of the trap once the cat has tripped the trap's mechanism and has become confined within the trap.
- Remember to put the trapped cat inside the vehicle with you. It is not a good idea to put a scared feral cat into the trunk of the car. The movements that happen in the trunk of the car due to the travel of the car on the road terrifies the cat.
- Take the cats as directly as possible to the vet or a neuter clinic. Talk to the vet beforehand letting them know what you are doing. Because you are

going to release the cats back into the wild you need to make sure that the clinic only uses dissolvable sutures as a part of the surgery process. You will not likely be able to go through the time and expense of re-trapping the animal so that they can go to the vet a second time to have stiches removed.

CHAPTER FOUR: Post Surgery

- The cats are always returned back to you in the same traps. You should also get a file with their medical records and the vaccines given. Keep all of these records safe. You never know when you might need them.
- Keep the cats indoors through the night (maybe in a basement, garage, or spare bathroom). The cats will come home in the traps in which you took them to the vet. They will remain in their traps until they are released again into the wild. Having the right setup will help your furry little friend be calm once the anaesthesia wears off.
- You need to keep a continuous watch over the cats for any kind of bleeding or infection.
- Do not take the cats outside while they are under your care. They might cause a nuisance to your neighbours. There have been cases where these cats have killed or injured small animal life around them.

- Once the cat regains consciousness, give them some water. Kittens can be fed immediately after they regain consciousness. However, you need to wait for about 8 hours before you feed the adult cat with solid food. Make sure you do not open the trap very much at all while feeding the cat. Chances are, they might find this as an opportunity to attack you and run out of the trap. The trap should only be opened just enough to let in the food and water.

CHAPTER FIVE: Return

In normal cases, a cat needs about 24 hours to recover. After that, they can be returned back to their original location. Ensure that all the cats are completely conscious and alert before they are returned to their original site.

Once you get the trap at the site, open the trap door and walk away. Do not get worried if the cat takes some time to come out of the trap. She is getting reacquainted with her original surroundings.

Do not relocate the cat unless it is absolutely necessary. Relocate the cat only if its life is endangered by other feral cats in the vicinity or if the location of the whole colony is being moved together.

DO'S AND DONT'S

Some things you must always be careful to do:

- Keep the emergency number of the veterinarian handy at all times.
- Choose a clinic close to your home.
- Keep the trapped cats in places which is free of pollution and noise
- Purchase a first-aid kit for yourself and your helpers. Your health is important! Trapping a feral cat is not easy. Many people involved in TNR will tell you (or show you) that injuries, such as scratches and bites are commonplace in the practice of trapping ferals. This is why, if you decide to get involved with TNR programs, it is recommended that you go for tetanus injections which should generally be administered every 5 years. Rabies shots should also be considered if you often deal with any wild animals which could possibly carry the virus.

Some things you must not do:

- Do not leave the traps unattended.
- Ensure that you do not pet or touch the cats while they are inside the traps. I realize that they are cute, but petting them could endanger your safety.

CHAPTER SIX: Sheltering Feral Cats

Almost all feral cats, though very resourceful, cannot survive the cold. They do have thickened coats that keep them a little warm during the day. But the night time when the temperature drops is when they need human help. Feral cats as well as outside/outdoor cats need warm, dry and size-appropriate shelters that help them survive the cold weather

There are a few shelters that can house one cat at one time. However, in a colony, having just one cat per shelter does not make sense. Though ferals are shy of humans, most of them take care of the members of the rest of the colony. This just means that you can have a shelter that houses more than 3-4 cats at a time.

It is our suggestion that you avoid shelters that are made of plastic. You don't live in plastic, neither should a helpless animal.

Find shelters that are made of wood. It is a natural, eco-friendly material that cats have a natural affinity toward.

For people that are handy with a hammer and a saw (and have no need for style or aesthetics) there are a number of designs for cat shelters online.

However, for many people the thrown together / homemade look is simply not appealing. The cats don't care, but the neighbours do! In many municipalities it is necessary to house feral cats in shelters/houses that look neat and tidy so as not to affect the ambiance and property values of the neighbourhood.

Because of this, we suggest that any colony in a populated area be supplied with cat houses and food shelters from www.thecathousestore.com This company offers an array of pre-insulated outdoor cedar cat houses and food shelters that are appropriate for the cats and attractive to the passerby. They even have an option for heated houses and shelters! One advantage of buying and using shelters from The Cat

House Store is that they have a uniform appearance and your shelters don't look haphazard or thrown together. This makes cats cozy and neighbours happy!

If you plan on making a shelter, ensure that the shelter is big enough to house 3-4 cats, but small enough so that the heat from the cat's body does not escape from the shelter. A shelter that is too small will restrict the movement of the cat. If the shelter is too big, the cat's body heat will not keep the space warm thereby rendering the shelter useless.

Although cat shelters can be made, a few companies make cat shelters that are already well insulated and come with a warranty. If you do not want to take the trouble of making a shelter, you can always buy one of these. They last well and are worth the investment.

Some do's in regard to houses/shelters:

Straw is the best option that can be put inside a cat shelter. The cats burrow into the straw and it acts as insulation to help them stay warm in the cold nights. If straw is not available, pillow cases with shredded newspaper should do the trick. In extreme weather conditions, cover the walls and the floor of the cat house with Mylar. These plastic sheets will trap the heat of the cat in the cat house, ensuring, the cat is warm at all times.

In placing the shelters on site remember that each shelter should be kept about a foot or two apart from each other. They should be heavy enough to withstand a winter's wind and may need to be put onto stilts or a platform to allow for snowfall. The doors of the houses should face each other. That way, the cat will be able to find an empty space for itself without fighting it out with other cats.

Ensure that you keep the shelters clean at all times. Replace the straw and newspaper whenever they are dirty, soiled or moist. Wash and re-stuff the pillowcases as and when required.

Some don'ts in regard to houses/shelters:

Make sure you do not put blankets, towels, used clothing or folded newspaper as an insulation for the shelter. The cat cannot burrow itself under any of them. As a result, these materials suck up the body heat from the cat. Hay is also not a good option because it is made up of different kinds of plant life. Hay may poke and irritate the cat and it might become allergic to the plant life in the hay.

Make sure you never put food or water inside the shelter. The food might attract scavengers like raccoons or wild dogs. This will cause a commotion between the wild animals getting the cats stressed. The water might spill in the shelter endangering the health of the cats inside the shelter. Instead we recommend building a separate shelter for the food and water. Again, you can build your own, but to have one that is pleasing to the eye and coordinates well with your houses is important for peace within the neighbourhood. It is because of this, and because of their commitment to high quality houses and food shelters for feral and outside cats we recommend again TheCatHouseStore.com. There you will find several sizes of food shelters that will coordinate with the houses/shelters that they sell.

CHAPTER SEVEN: Feeding Feral Cats

Food is something that develops a bond between the caretaker and the feral cat. Though feral cats are wary of humans, the food will help the cat dissolve the fear and will learn to appreciate the caretaker.

Feral cats normally kill and eat mice, rats, and small birds that are around the neighbourhood and because of this they are productive to have around. These cats also relish raw fish. Most of the time, however raw fish is well out of the price range to feed to cats. If you do live in a fishing area where you can obtain fish to feed to the cats please do keep an eye on them as fish can sometimes upset their stomachs. You can always treat them to a cooked or canned fish anytime.

Cats love meat. Along with the taste, they also need the protein for a strong heart and good eyesight. Cooked beef, chicken and fish will give the cat all the nutrition they require. In case of financial constraints, you can also give the cat oats and brown rice, wheat, and barley. However, you would need to mash them up before you give them to the cat.

Eggs are also nutritious. However, you need to ensure that the eggs are completely cooked before feeding them to the cats.

Veggies are also a great source of food. However, like most human kids, cats do not like the taste of veggies or fruits. The next option here is to mix it along with their fish food.

Cats should not be given foods like chocolate, grapes, raisins, onions, garlic, bread dough, and alcohol. I don't know who was getting their cats drunk, but if it was you, STOP IT! (Ha! Ha!) If the cats eat any of the above, you can rest assured that you will be visiting your vet very soon.

The cats eat everything that we as humans do. You do not have to really make the effort of cooking something especially for the cat. These cats will happily gorge on whatever food you give them. Cats are not fussy.

Now that we have said that cats like the kind of food that we do, we also understand that finances do not allow us to feed feral cats with the same food that we feed ourselves. It is perfectly acceptable to feed your feral cats a store bought cat food. They will naturally supplement whatever you feed them with the spoils of their days hunting adventures.

Though the kind of food you give them may not be an issue, you need to take care of the way you give them their food.

You need to make sure that the feeding station / food shelter is located close to the shelter so that the cat does not have to travel too far for food. (see feeding stations at TheCatHouseStore.com)

Since Feral cats do not like the company of humans, it is better to keep the feeding station in a place that has no traffic and minimal human interaction.

Do not go for any fancy food bowls. Ask around for steel containers. If steel ones are not available, any containers that do not have sharp edges and are unbreakable should be useful. Know the number of cats in a colony and organize the number of bowls accordingly. For example one might purchase and set up one bowl for about 3 cats. Maintain some distance between bowls to reduce the chances of fighting among cats.

Make sure you get a large bowl only for water, and refill the water every day. Sometimes the well-meaning people who feed feral cats forget to give their cat colony water. When you forget to give the feral cats water they tend to venture further away from the colony site in search of water and can get into trouble or into situations that endanger their lives.

The best time to replace food and water is at dusk. Traffic is minimal at this hour. This timing also helps the food from spoiling in the sun. Since cats are nocturnal animals (they like the night), they will not have problems having their meal in the dark.

Since feral cats are not generally human friendly, they will not come near a food bowl if you are around. Once you serve them food, back off and let the cats enjoy the sumptuous food you have brought to them. Once they learn to trust you, their mannerisms will change. They will come out and look expectantly at the bowls that are in your hand.

Establish a signal for the cats to show them that it is feeding time. It can be a whistle, song, or tinkling bell that you use during the placing of the food. To start with, start the signal while you serve them so that they learn to associate that signal with food. Along with improving your vocal chords, the cats will be able to associate the food with its giver. You, on the other hand, will be able to see the increase or decrease in cats and also check out for the ones who need to go through the TNR process.

The best place to keep the food for feral cats is in feeding stations or food shelters that keep out the rain. Turn the shelters so that they face each other.

Ensure that you clean and disinfect every bowl every time you feed the cats. You need to wash your hands with a sanitizer every time you come in contact with these cats. This is for your protection.

Once you are committed to being a caretaker for a feral cat colony, make sure that you stand by your commitment. Cats have an acute sense of timing. They will expect you to come with food at the appointed hour. If you plan to go on a vacation, ask your neighbour to take your place. The other option is that you can ask your local animal rescue organization to feed the cats when you are away. If they are agreeable to helping, they will send a volunteer every night at the appointed hour to feed the cats that you have neutered.

CHAPTER EIGHT: Health Care Essentials for Feral Cats

Cats, by nature, do not need a lot of attention. All they need is food, shelter, health, a little affection and they are as happy as a child with ice cream. Feral cats are especially easy to handle as they thrive in the wild and do not require human affection.

DISEASES

Cats, especially feral and stray, are known for parasites like roundworms, hookworms, coccidian and tapeworms. They can prove fatal to the cat. Deworming medications that can be bought through your local vet come to the rescue. These medications can be mixed with wet food and given to the cats. This should take care of these parasites. Fleas can be controlled by medications like Frontline or Revolution. If necessary while the cat is under anaesthesia, you can apply topical medication.

Though feral cats are prone to diseases like rabies, it is unlikely that this will be passed on to humans. The reason being, that feral cats shy away from humans. So, unless provoked, these cats do not bite. Research says that almost 90% of the cat bites were provoked. You also need to remember that most of the TNR programs also cover rabies vaccinations.

FIV (Feline Immunodeficiency Syndrom) is very similar to HIV in humans. It is transmitted primarily through bites and scratches occurring during fights. Unlike HIV in humans, FIV is very rarely transmitted through sexual contact. It can also be transmitted to kittens if an FIV mother cat gives birth. The life expectancy of cats with FIV is around 5 years, although it may vary depending on the general health and genetics of the cat. Trapping and sterilising of feral cats is therefore of great importance, to minimise the risk of both transmission from mothers to kittens, as well as minimising the risk of male cats fighting and transmitting through this.

The most common way humans can contact any disease from the cats is through the cat feces. However, if the volunteer practices sanitization, the risk of getting infected are almost nothing.

MYTHS

A number of people advocate euthanizing feral cats instead of replacing them into the wild. Their faulty reasons are:

Pet animals get life threatening diseases due to feral cats. However, these diseases could never be directly linked to feral cats. There are a number of wild animals all over the place where pet animals can get diseases from.

Feral cats can carry toxoplasmosis. Another disease that may spread from a feral cat to another animal is toxoplasmosis. However, these diseases come from uncooked food that the feral cat might feed on. So, if the cat is fed nutritious and healthy food, the chances of getting toxoplasmosis reduces to a great extent.

Feral cats carry fleas. Cats are not the only reason fleas are around. Yes, fleas feed on cats and live on them as well. However, if you remove cats, the fleas will find another source to feed themselves on. Fleas can thrive on any source that has hair, is unkept, and wild. So, a racoon, a dog, or a squirrel can become the next source.

People around the world need to remember that if any of the accusations were true, those taking care of these colonies of cats would be infected by these diseases. The fact that all these caregivers are as fit as a fiddle, proves that all these accusations are baseless. This is where education about a feral cat can prove useful.

CHAPTER NINE: The Right Mindset for Humans in Caring for Feral Cats

People prefer taking care of domestic cats rather than feral cats. The reason is that domestic cats are trained animals who are free of danger or disease. Domestic cats, with their playful activities, can entertain you to no end. They climb onto your lap and want you to pet them. Most important....They are extremely affectionate and show it!

Ferals, being shy of humans, fear human proximity and human contact. An adult feral cat might take months, or even years to tame. Most of them will never be tamed. The chances of a feral allowing you to pet them or allowing you to remain near them are very small. In fact, there is some danger in attempting to pet a feral cat. You must remember that these are wild animals in your care not pets in your home. You must have the mentality of a kind and loving zookeeper.

The caretaker must combat a number of issues while they save and take care of these cats. Some of them are:

> Emergency relocation of cats and kittens due to sickness, starvation and security
> Exhausting personal funds due to veterinary and caretaking expenditures
> Inability to purchase the required food due to lack of funds
> Inadequate shelters and feeding stations during the winter months
> Travelling long distances to feed feral cats

A number of human beings, after a certain point of time, feel frustrated as they feel that their work bears no fruit, and that they do not get love in return.

However, those who really want to do these cats some good, know the psychological barriers. They continue to serve the cats for the rest of the cat's life without expecting any love in return. They consider it a life changing moment if the feral cat becomes friends with them. They feel good that the feral has found the confidence to trust them. It just shows that the patience has been rewarded.

If you want to adopt a feral, it's best to adopt a feral kitten rather than a fully grown feral cat. The kitten will take anywhere between 2 days to 2 weeks to become completely tame. You need to allow them to grow accustomed to having you around them. Ensure you feed them at the same time every day. Put a few treats every day on a worn sweatshirt or a T-shirt that smells like you so they understand you are a treat man/woman. This way, they get familiar with your scent and, in due course, will get accustomed to you being around them. Talk to them about whatever you are doing without trying to go near them. You can also try reading a book or sleeping in the same room. In due course, they will realize that you mean no threat to them. They will be the ones who will want to know you better and will come to you. Once that happens, you and the cat are bonded for life.

Conclusion

Thank you again for buying this book!

I hope this book was able to help you to learn more about the process of helping a feral cat colony.

The next step is to network with other cat lovers in your area and make a plan to help these needy animals!

Finally, if you enjoyed this book, then I'd like to ask you for a favor. Would you be kind enough to leave a review for this book on Amazon or Amazon Kindle Store? It'd be greatly appreciated!

Thank you and good luck!

- *Carol-Ann Kennedy*

.

We invite you to visit <u>The Cat House Store.com</u>! We care about feral cats and the overpopulation problem facing our communities. That is why we have lent our support to and sponsored the publishing of this important informational book.

We sell cat houses and food shelters made only of high quality outdoor cedar wood. We have the house to keep your feral cats dry, warm and happy! Your cat's new home can come in many different styles. We offer everything from a small house big enough for just one outdoor cat to stacked houses and duplexes for those that are serious about rescuing and caring for the feral cats in their community.

We are all about getting you what you want for your cat.

We care about our product. This is the house that you would design and build for your cat if you had the time, skills, and resources to build it yourself. So go ahead, get your cat the home of its dreams, then both you and your feline friend will rest easy at night.

www.TheCatHouseStore.com

Made in the USA
Las Vegas, NV
05 November 2024

11185446R00026